THE SOCIAL COMPASS CURRICULUM

FLASHCARD SET

- Body Language Binoculars
- Proximity Compass
- Voice-o-Meter
- Glance Gauge
- Emotional Climate Map
- Emotional Intensity Indicator
- Empathy Footprint
- Positive Headset
- Relevance Radar
- Trail Marker
- GPS Alert
- Self-Portrait
- Handle
- Self-Controller
- Membership Card
- Start Button
- Question Bubble
- Display Case
- Compliment Confetti
- Interest Inventory
- Paraphrasing Funnel
- Friendship Balance
- Conversation Glue
- Time's-Up Tin

SCCFC

Contents

1 summary card

4 introduction cards (1 for each of 4 modules):

- NONVERBAL SKILLS
- EMOTIONS
- SOCIAL PROBLEM SOLVING
- "WE" SKILLS

24 individual visual support cards

MODULE 1

NONVERBAL SKILLS

MODULE 1

NONVERBAL SKILLS

Body Language Binoculars

Body Language Binoculars

Binoculars help people see images that are far away. Body Language Binoculars help us see other people's body language without attending to the words they speak. We can make a determination about what they are communicating based on the gestures and stances they take.

Proximity Compass

Proximity Compass

The Proximity Compass is a reminder to think of concentric circles for the distance people stand from each other depending on which relationship circle they belong to. "Self" is in the middle circle, followed by family, friends, acquaintances, and strangers. We have corresponding behaviors for each.

HUG—HANDSHAKE—WAVE—NO CONTACT

Voice-o-Meter

Voice-o-Meter

Like a thermometer that rises when it heats up, the Voice-o-Meter shows the volume level or tone of voice we are using. Each level has an appropriate use in particular settings.

Glance Gauge

Glance Gauge

Like a timer, the Glance Gauge indicates the length of someone's eye contact with another—which is also called social referencing. A glance is for gathering quick information, a longer look indicates wanting to be included, and a stare indicates intense feelings.

MODULE 2

EMOTIONS

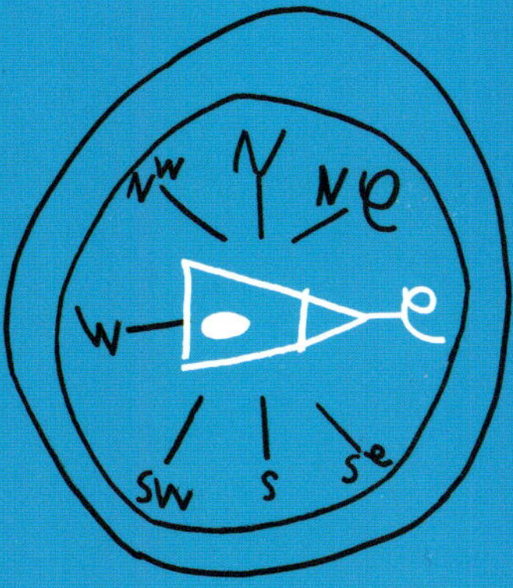

MODULE 2

EMOTIONS

Emotional Climate Map

Emotional Climate Map

Like a weather map, the Emotional Climate Map provides a forecast or reading of the mood of the group at a particular moment or in a specific circumstance. Group mood, or a group's emotional climate, has a huge impact on our behavior. Reading the map correctly is important.

Emotional Intensity Indicator

Emotional Intensity Indicator

Like a ruler that measures how long something is, the Emotional Intensity Indicator measures how intense our reactions are to a given situation. We want to keep "in measure" with the situation so that we demonstrate appropriate social responses.

Empathy Footprint

Empathy Footprint

The Empathy Footprint reminds us to put ourselves in someone else's shoes and feel what that person might be feeling.

Positive Headset

Positive Headset

In difficult situations, a positive mind-set is an important skill. The Positive Headset reminds us to play positive tapes to ourselves—also known has having positive self-talk—and to shift emotional states when needed by social circumstance.

MODULE 3

SOCIAL PROBLEM SOLVING

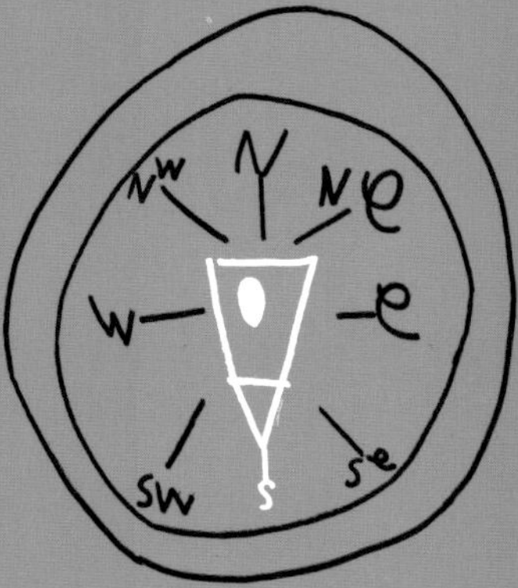

MODULE 3

SOCIAL PROBLEM SOLVING

Relevance Radar

Relevance Radar

Keeping our comments related to the discussion topic becomes concrete when we see on a radar map exactly where our comments are related to the central topic. We can use the reading on the radar to see if we are on topic or off the map. Watching others' body language can provide feedback on topic boundary errors.

Trail Marker

Trail Marker

When we are on a hiking path and get lost, we refer to the trail markers to get back on track. If we are not paying attention to the group, we can recall the Trail Marker visual support and request information about our location (e.g., "I'm sorry—what did you say?").

GPS
Alert

GPS Alert

Sometimes unexpected changes happen. In our car, a GPS can alert us when traffic patterns change and can provide a different route. When we are alerted to a change, we acknowledge the change and begin to move on with a plan. We all have a GPS in our minds, or we can work out a new plan with the group (GPS = Group Problem Solver).

Self-Portrait

Self-Portrait

This is a picture of an important person. In the picture frame is you. The frame around your face provides a container for where your focus should be. This image is designed as a reminder to pay attention to your needs and not anyone else's. A self-portrait contains you, the person you need to monitor. Rather than tattle on others, the Self-Portrait visual support is a reminder to focus on yourself—or to mind your own business.

Handle

Handle

Sometimes, losing control of our emotions is called "flying off the handle." The point of holding onto a handle is to gain or maintain control. When we steer a bike, we have the most control when our hands are on the handle bars. When we feel like we might fly off the handle, the Handle is there to remind us to grab on and get a grip.

Self-Controller

Self-Controller

Like a remote to turn the TV on or off, the Self-Controller helps us to hit the "stop" button when we get angry. It is better to stop and think or walk away than to act out aggressive behavior. In real life, we cannot "undo" or "replay." Practicing our behavior in our minds before we act helps prevent the need to "undo" our actions.

Membership Card

Membership Card

This card indicates membership in the group. When we want to belong to a group, we apply to be a member and agree to follow the group's rules. We may then get a card that shows our membership. In life, we might get left out, and we need to remember to communicate our desire to be included. We need to seek membership.

MODULE 4

"WE" SKILLS

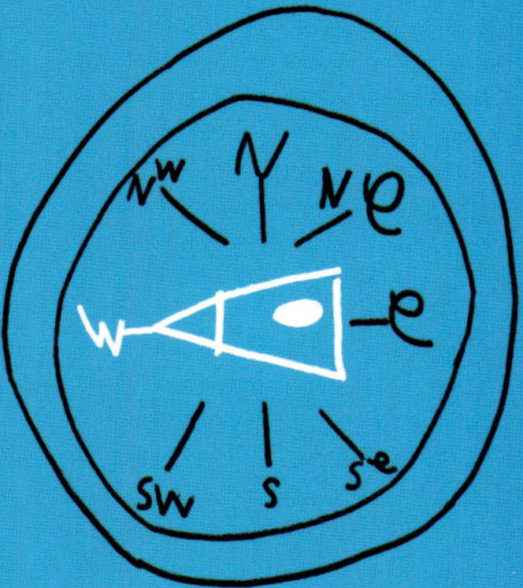

MODULE 4

"WE" SKILLS

Start Button

Start Button

To turn on a computer, we push the start button. Without pushing this button, there is no power. To begin a conversation, we need to push a start button to get the conversation going. Just push it to begin. Nothing starts without first pushing the power button, so go ahead and push the Start Button.

Question Bubble

Question Bubble

In comics, bubbles appear above the characters' heads to share their thoughts or dialogue. When we want to keep a conversation going or want to gather more information, the Question Bubble reminds us to ask questions to get answers.

Display Case

Display Case

We all have interests. The display case reminds us to share our talents and knowledge with others to help them get to know us better. They might find our interests interesting, too.

Compliment Confetti

Compliment Confetti

Confetti represents a celebration or party. When we compliment a person, he or she might get a happy feeling—and that is a good thing.

Interest Inventory

Interest Inventory

To stay current and useful, we check our inventory of interests. Are we expanding our inventory, keeping track of all we know and where we want to add more information? Our knowledge must get updated regularly, too. The Interest Inventory reminds us to check and see what we can learn about next.

Paraphrasing Funnel

Paraphrasing Funnel

To show we are actively listening and understanding someone's message, we summarize it using the overall concept or most important words. We do not echo back the exact words, which would sound insincere. The Paraphrasing Funnel helps us to sift through the words to find the meaning.

Friendship Balance

Friendship Balance

Friendship is demonstrated by taking turns, having reciprocal interactions, sharing experiences, sharing a goal, and having joint attention. The Friendship Balance reminds us to keep it even to be sure we are reciprocating, thus keeping a balance in our friendship.

Conversation Glue

Conversation Glue

Glue holds things together; Conversation Glue keeps our comments stuck to the topic. We need to be sure we have applied glue in our minds so our responses stick. Conversation Glue is made up of words that relate to or connect two thoughts or statements together.

Time's-Up Tin

Time's-Up Tin

To be good citizens, we clean up our trash by putting it in a trash can. When a conversation ends, we need to be sure we neatly wrap up our conversations and put them away. Sometimes our time is up before we are done, and we need to respect that constraint. We also synchronize when we wrap up while talking in a group—we don't throw our trash away and leave until everyone is done. The Time's-Up Tin helps us monitor others to see when they are done or when our time is up so that we can coordinate this ending together.

SCCFC